Watching
Bison
in North America

L. Patricia Kite

Heinemann Library
Chicago, Illinois

Customer Service 888-454-2279
Visit our website at www.heinemannlibrary.com

Designed by Ron Kamen and edesign
Illustrations by Martin Sanders
Printed and bound in China by South China Printing Company Limited

10 09 08 07 06
10 9 8 7 6 5 4 3 2 1

Library of Congress Cataloging-in-Publication Data
Kite, L. Patricia.
  Watching bison in North America / L. Patricia Kite.
    p. cm. -- (Wild world)
  Includes bibliographical references.
  ISBN 1-4034-7232-7 (library binding - hardcover : alk. paper) -- ISBN 1-4034-7245-9 (pbk. : alk. paper)
  1. American bison--North America--Juvenile literature. I. Title. II. Series: Wild world (Chicago, Ill.)
  QL737.U53K59 2006
  599.64'3'097--dc22
                            2005016 10

Acknowledgments
The author and publishers are grateful to the following for permission to reproduce copyright material: Ardea p. 11 (Francois Gohier), 15 (Francois Gohier), 16 (S. Roberts), 17 (Tom and Pat Leeson), 23 (Francois Gohier); Corbis pp. 7, 21, 22, 27; FLPA pp. 13, 14, 24; Getty Images p. 26 (Hulton Archive); Nature Picture Library pp. 4 (David Kjaer), 5 (Jose Ruiz), 8 (Ingo Arndt), 9 (Ingo Arndt), 10 (Herman Brehm), 18 (Thomas Lazar), 19 (Mary Ann McDonald), 20 (Ingo Arndt). Cover photograph of bison reproduced with permission of Corbis (Kennan Ward).

Dedicated to Samuel and Daniel Raney.

The publishers would like to thank Michael Bright of the BBC Natural History Unit for his assistance in the preparation of this book.Every effort has been made to contact copyright holders of any material reproduced in this book. Any omissions will be rectified in subsequent printings if notice is given to the publisher. The paper used to print this book comes from sustainable resources.

Some words are shown in bold, **like this**. You can find out what they mean by looking in the glossary.

Contents

Meet the Bison

This is North America, the home of bison. Bison are **mammals**. An adult **male** may be as big as a small truck.

▼ *Bison travel across the* ***continent*** *in* ***herds***.

Bison live in North America and Europe. Some people call them buffalo, but that is wrong. Buffalo are a different kind of animal.

Buffalo live in Africa and Asia.

At Home in North America

The **continent** of North America is huge. It has many different **landscapes**. There are mountains and deserts. There are valleys and **prairies**.

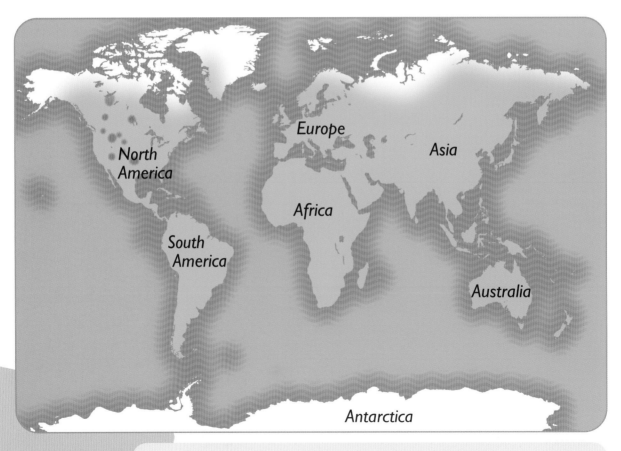

Key ● *This color shows where bison live in North America.*

▲ *Bison need lots of open space to live.*

Bison roam the prairies and river valleys. There are few trees here. Many grasses grow for bison to eat.

7

There's a Bison!

Bison are easy to spot on the flat **prairies**. They are large animals with horns and four legs. They have dark fur and a woolly beard to match.

▶▶ *A bison's huge head makes it look even wider.*

*Both **male** and **female** bison have horns.*
Males are called bulls.

horns

hump

tail

beard

legs

The bison has a large hump above its
shoulders. This makes it look even taller.
Its thin tail has a brush-shaped tuft at
the end.

9

Meal Time

The bison spend most of the day **grazing**. Their favorite foods are grasses. They also eat twigs and leaves. They visit a **water hole** to drink.

Finding water is just as important as finding food.

The bison swallow their food quickly. They do not chew it much at first. Later, the food travels back up into their mouths so they can chew it more.

▲ The partly-chewed food is called **cud**. Bison chew it as they rest.

On the Move

Bison travel slowly, in small groups. Sometimes they gather together in a large **herd**. If just one bison starts running, the whole herd might **stampede**.

▶▶ *The pounding **hooves** of a large herd make a sound like thunder.*

Bison are good swimmers. When they come to a river, they go right in. Bison also use water to keep clean and to wash insects away.

A bison swims with its head and hump above water.

Life in Winter

In winter, freezing winds and storms blow across the **prairies**. Snow covers trees, bushes, and grass. A bison's thick winter fur keeps it warm.

▲ *Bison grow extra fur for the cold winters.*

Finding food takes extra work in winter.
Grasses are hidden under the snow.
The bison swings its head to push the
snow away.

▼ *A bison uses its nose like a snowplow.*

Springtime Shedding

In spring, the weather warms up. The bison's thick winter fur falls off in large patches. The warm weather also brings flies. They bite the bison.

Sometimes bare skin shows when a bison sheds.

The bites itch, so bison roll back and forth on soft ground. They get covered in mud and dust. This helps make the bites feel better.

⬆ *Dust rolling helps bison shed fur and cool off.*

Mating Time

Bison look for **mates** in late summer. If two bulls like the same **female**, a fight may start. The bulls paw the ground and roar.

▼ *Bulls make a bellowing sound to attract females.*

The bison run toward each other.
A shoving match begins. The strongest
bull wins. He goes to stand next to his
chosen female.

There is a loud crash as their
heads bump together.

Bison Babies

Bison babies are born in the spring, nine months after **mating**. Each **female** gives birth to just one calf. The calf is a reddish color.

▲ *Bison calves drink their mothers' milk.*

Within minutes, the calf tries to stand. At first it falls down, but soon it can run. If the **herd** begins to run, the calf must be able to keep up.

▼ *Young calves are shaky on their legs.*

Growing Up

The mothers watch over their calves. They make soft grunting noises if a calf wanders away. The calf answers with high-pitched squeals.

▲ *Bison calves soon learn to eat grass.*

Growing calves pretend to fight and butt heads.

At two months old, a calf begins to grow its hump and horns. The horns start as tiny fur-covered bumps. The calves like to chase each other.

Enemies

Bison are in danger from mountain lions, bears, wolves, and coyotes. If a **predator** is nearby, the adults make a circle. They protect the calves.

▶▶ *A bison calf would be a tasty meal for a mountain lion.*

People also cause problems for bison. Bison are killed for sport or meat. They lose their homes when **prairies** are cleared to make room for houses and cattle.

▲ *Today bison must share the prairies with people.*

Saving the Bison

Long ago, there were millions of bison. Native Americans hunted them. They did not kill more than they needed. Then, **settlers** came and killed many bison.

Native Americans used bison for food, clothing, and shelter.

By 1890, bison were almost **extinct**. Parks were set up where bison could live in peace. Today, bison live on private land and in national parks.

Now there are many thousands of bison in North America.

Tracker's Guide

When you want to watch animals in the wild, you need to find them first. You can look for clues they leave behind.

▲ *Bison leave piles of droppings behind as they move across the **prairies**.*

◀◀ If you find bison fur caught on a tree trunk, it means that a bison has used the tree to scratch.

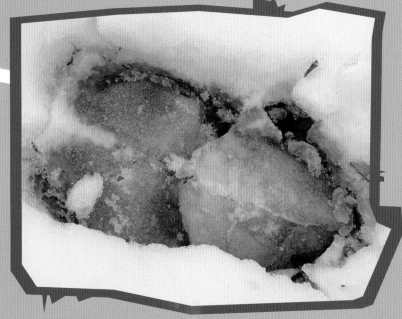

▶▶ You can track bison by tracks left in mud and snow.

Glossary

continent the world is split into seven large areas of land called continents. Each continent is divided into different countries.

cud partly-chewed food

extinct has died out forever

female animal that can become a mother when it is grown up. Girls and women are female people.

graze to eat grass

herd large group of grass-eating animals

hoof hard covering on the feet of some animals

landscape type of landforms found in a place. A landscape can have mountains, rivers, forests, and many other things.

male animal that can become a father when it is grown up. Boys and men are male people.

mammal animal that feeds its babies with the mother's milk

mate when male and female animals produce young. "Mate" can also mean the partner that an animal has babies with.

prairie wide, grassy plain with few trees

predator animal that catches and eats other animals for food

settler person who comes to live in a new country or place

stampede to run away quickly in a large group

water hole pool where animals go to drink water

Find Out More

Books

Fox, Mary Virginia. *North America*. Chicago: Heinemann Library, 2001.

Ganeri, Anita. *Animal Life Cycles*. Chicago: Heinemann Library, 2005.

Stone, Lynn M. *Bison*. Vero Beach, Fla.: Rourke Publishing, 2003.

Whitehouse, Patricia. *Plains*. Chicago: Heinemann Library, 2005.

An older reader can help you with these books:

Becker, John. *The American Bison*. Farmington Hills, Mich.: Gale Group, 2003.

Pyers, Greg. *Why Am I a Mammal?* Chicago: Raintree, 2005.

Quigley, Mary. *Prairie Explorer*. Chicago: Raintree, 2005.

Randolph, Ryan P. *Following the Great Herds: The Plains Indians and the American Buffalo*. New York: Rosen, 2003.

Index